Yet Will I Trust Him

Bible Study on the Book of Job

Ricky LaVaughn

Yet Will I Trust Him: Bible Study on the Book of Job

Copyright 2015

Published by LaVauri Publishing House

Printed in the United States of America

www.lavauri.com

Cover Designed by Ricky LaVaughn

Other Bible Studies by Ricky LaVaughn

In The Beginning: Bible Study on the Book of Genesis

Foundation of the Fire

For more information on this book go to:

https://www.lavauri.com/yetwillitrusthim.html

Acknowledgements

I have to give a special thank you to my Grandmother, Ann C. Gray. She was my editor for the book and helped make this a wonderful and correct Bible Study to explore. Also, have to say thank you to Pastor Yuliyan Filipov for his direction and guidance in leading me to finding the information for this Study.

Table of Contents

Introduction

The book of Job. What an interesting, complicated, emotional, and poetic book this is. The idea to write this Bible Study after "In The Beginning" came because I erroneously assumed that the story and life of Job happened before the Great Flood. I'm not sure where that came from (possibly because this is considered the oldest book written in the Bible), but it is what I believed at the time. It didn't take long to learn the truth. Instead, by talking with Pastor Yuliyan Filipov and research, it is widely believe that Moses in fact wrote this book during his exile period. He wrote the book of Job first before writing Genesis and the rest of the Pentateuch.

Job is mostly a wisdom book written in the style of poetry. What makes this different then most Biblical books is that it is told as a conversation amongst friends. One of them is suffering (Job) while the others discuss his source of pain. Is the suffering due to an outside source, wicked people, God, or Job himself? These ideas are some of the factors mentioned between the men.

My goal while writing this Bible Study and many others in the future is to not go heavy with doctrine, denominational beliefs, traditions, and personal ideas. Of course, by writing the book some of my background and ideals will filter into the written words. The best-case scenario is to allow you the ability to read Job and have a personal understanding of the book as you pray for understanding and application.

When reading Job, think of it as a metaphor in listening and talking. If you're talking while someone else is speaking, often you can't understand or comprehend what they are saying. This is what we do when reading the Holy Bible. Our mind is metaphorically talking and blocking any information and truth that the Bible is speaking. When you're reading Job there is a conversation taking between the Bible and your mind. I implore you to listen to what the Word of God has to say. Don't approach learning more about the Lord as if you're trying to talk over the Scriptures. For many of us that sounds insane. If you have a desire to grow spiritually then you would never shout over the person who could provide instructions. Listen to what the Bible is saying. Then react and share with others.

The book of Job has 42 chapters and this study is broken into 26 lessons. Each lesson covers 1-2 chapters so you won't be over burden with reading too much information. In addition, each lesson is broken into three different sections. First, you have the questions relating to the Bible. After that, there will be personal questions for you to answer that relates to what you've just studied. Then the last section, Just a Thought, is a brief idea relating to the chapter for more information. Just a Thought is last so it doesn't color your mind while studying the lesson. Remember the idea is to have a blank slate going into each lesson of the Bible Study.

Something to think about before proceeding is that Job is full of metaphors. These examples are used to explain a variety of issues plaguing our world. Think about the people and community Job and his friends are describing and then think if that reflects the mindset and way of the world today. Really pay attention to what's being said. This is a conversation between people regarding suffering in the world on a personal and grand scale. Let's face it, we all suffer from some calamity or issue at some point in our lives.

By reading Job, the hope is that you will have a better grasp on how to view the situation and see how God is a part of your life.

The Beginning of the Calamities

Lesson 1

Job 1 - 2

1.)   Describe Job's character.

Job 1:1

2.)   What does the Bible say about Job's wealth?

Job 1:2-3

3.)   Describe Job's children and what did he do on their behalf?

Job 1:4-5

4.)   Who came to visit God?

Job 1:6-7

5.)   How does God describe Job?

Job 1:8

6.)   In Satan/Adversary's mind, why is Job being a good person? (Satan's title is often called adversary in various versions of the Bible.)

Job 1:9-11

7.)   What does God give Satan permission to do?

Job 1:12

8.)   What are the four calamities that happened to Job?

Job 1:13-19

9.)   What was Job's response to the trials?

Job 1:20-22

10.)   Divine beings and Satan came to present themselves for the Lord. What does God
         say about Job and what excuse does Satan give for his behavior?

Job 2:1-6

11.)   What was Job's next calamity? How did he respond?

Job 2:7-8

12.)   What did Job's wife suggest for him to do? What was his response?

Job 2:9-10

13.)   Who came to visit Job and how did they react upon seeing him?

Job 2:11-13

PERSONAL QUESTIONS

A.)   Often we help those who are constantly harming themselves. Why do you believe we do this and is there someone in your life that you're praying for or helping in spite of them harming themselves? (For example, a drug addict, being abusive, criminal behavior, gossiping, etc.)

B.)   Along with Satan, the book of Job mentions Divine beings presenting themselves before God. Who do you think they are and why are they coming?

C.)   Out of the calamities that happened to Job, which is the worst and why? Put yourself in his position when answering the question.

D.)   Often we forget that Job was married. How do you believe she felt to see her children, possessions, money, and husband all get destroyed or harmed? How would you feel if something similar happened to one of your family members?

E.)   God looked upon Job with favor knowing that he was an upright and great person. Why then would God allow extreme pain to come to a loyal servant?

JUST A THOUGHT

Unlike a variety of the prophetic books found in the Old Testament, as well as Paul's epistles and the Gospels found in the New, the book of Job does not mention an author. The book simply begins with the narrative to set the background for the poetic wisdom that will take up most of the scripture. The beginning is simply meant to set the stage so the reader will know the people, place, and calamities that will drive the book.

The most common belief is that Moses wrote Job. It's considered the oldest book of the Bible, not because of narrative timeframe (clearly that would make Genesis the oldest) but when it was actually written. Many scholars and religious leaders believe that Moses was impressed upon by God to write Job when he was in Midian. This was during a time of exile for him (Exodus 2:14-17), as he spent forty years away from Egypt. Midian is close to the land of Uz so it was likely that Moses heard the story of Job and used it as a means to teach others he was around. After all, just like the main character, Moses dealt with his own suffering as someone who lived in a palace to escaping and becoming a sheepherder.

Often times God is mentioned slightly different in Job compare to other books of the Bible. His name, Yahweh (YHWH) is rarely mentioned compare to Elohim. Also, God is referred to as Almighty often throughout the text.

Job lived between the time of Abraham and Moses. That's hundreds of years of history but remember this is something that takes place away from the main arc of characters we learn about at the end of Genesis (Isaac, Jacob, Joseph). Job lives to be 140 years old, which is a long time and could place him anywhere within that period.

To Never Be Born

Lesson 2

Job 3

1.)   What did Job say in response to his trials?

Job 3:1-3

2.)   What imagery did Job use for his birth?

Job 3:4-10

3)   What question was Job asking? Why do you believe he would have thoughts
on this subject?

Job 3:11-12

4.)   What existence was better than Job's current life? Whom would he have been
        with?

Job 3:13-15

5.)   Job compares untimely birth or miscarriage to freedom from problems. Who does
        Job believe has this freedom?

Job 3:16-19

6.)   To Job what are people given but search diligently for something else?

Job 3:20-22

7.)   Ultimately, what came for Job that he feared/dreaded?

Job 3:23-26

PERSONAL QUESTIONS

A.)   Considering Job's problems, how do you feel he responded? Do you agree or disagree with some of his thoughts? Explain.

B.)   Job had a mindset that not being born would be more tolerable then going through the pain/issue/problem that he suffered. Are there occasions when people are justified feeling this way? Are there situations when death appears to be a release? Please explain.

C.)   At the start of the Book of Job, it describes Job's life as being plush and full of wealth. His children were not up to standard so he often prayed from them. Why do you believe that going into hardship made Job feel like he never wanted to be born? Wishing for this would also mean that he wouldn't have experienced the great lifestyle he had previously.

D.)   Would it be better to have riches, power, and fame for all of that to be taken away; or never have those things in the first place?

JUST A THOUGHT

In this book, Job often talks about not being born. He used this phrase as a metaphor for wishing his current situation would end. The pain Job felt was so bad, that he either forgot or didn't consider that his life was full of wealth and huge blessings before his current situation.

Sometimes when going through pain, calamities, problems, or anything harming us, we often forget the good times. Like Job, we might use metaphors and descriptions to convey the pain that we're suffering. Even Jeremiah used a similar metaphor as Job when wishing for his painful situation to end (Jeremiah 20:18).

Do not get Job's mindset confused with suicide. He didn't want to kill himself. If you have thoughts of suicide or a desire to take your life, please pray for strength and call the National Suicide Prevention Lifeline. They're open constantly and can be of help. Please visit the website or call below for assistance and help.

National Suicide Prevention Lifeline

800-273-8255

www.suicidepreventionlifeline.org

Eliphaz's Encouraging Words

Lesson 3

Job 4-5

1.)   How does Eliphaz start his response?

Job 4:1-2

2.)   Name a few things that Job has done for others.

Job 4:3-4

3.)   Eliphaz state that innocent and righteous people will not be destroyed. Describe the
       metaphor he uses for how sinners will be treated.

Job 4:5-11

4.)   Describe Eliphaz's vision.

Job 4:12-17

5.)   What is Eliphaz explanation of his vision/dream?

Job 4:18-21

6.)   What are some of the people and problems that Eliphaz list?

Job 5:1-7

7.)   What advice is given to Job and why?

Job 5:8

8.)   List some of the things God does for people.

Job 5:9-16

9.)   There is a multitude of calamities that Eliphaz states God will use to correct a
        person's behavior. What are a few of them?

Job 5:17-20

10.)   Eliphaz encourages Job by talking about various great events that will happen.
        Name a few of them.

Job 5:21-27

PERSONAL QUESTIONS

A.)   To Eliphaz, God doesn't just dispatch justice, but blesses people as well, (Job 5:9-16). What does this reveal about God's character?

B.)   Is it possible for cities to influence who we are as a person why or why not?

C.)   Think about the city you're living in and how has it influenced your mindset and behavior?

D.)   Think about a family member or friend that you would want to give advice or encouraging words. After writing it down, call, text, email, or communicate this to them.

JUST A THOUGHT

Eliphaz is one of Job's friends who lived in a part of Edom called Teman. During the time of Job, there were nations but it wasn't quite what we have now. They had groups of clans and families all working for one purpose and goal. The Israelites, for example, were a nation of 12 tribes unified by God. Edom was similar and had it's origin in Esau, Jacob's brother.

Esau at first held a grudge against his brother for stealing his birthright (Genesis 25:29-34) and blessing (Genesis 27:1-41) but then made amends (Genesis 33:1-17). Esau ended up having a large family himself with many sons by a variety of wives and concubines. The eldest of his children was Eliphaz who had a son named Teman. The eventual tribe, Temanites, which came out of Eliphaz, was named after Teman who became a power that are often called Edom or Edomites.

The Eliphaz that is mentioned in Job is not the same person as Esau's eldest son. He did come out of the Temanite people and was probably an important person or the eldest of his family for his dad to give him the name of a prominent person from their clan. This means that Eliphaz had some sway, power, and at least wealth. This isn't out of the ordinary since most people associate with those who are on a similar level. Job was a very wealthy person so he would have similar associates and friends.

Eliphaz have a very well defined view of God. To him there is good and evil and the Lord blesses and punishes according to your deeds and actions. With this viewpoint Eliphaz is of course looking at Job figuring that for his friend to go through such a horrible trial, certainly Job had to of done something wrong.

You Don't Know, Like I Know

Lesson 4

Job 6-7

1.)   What metaphor does Job use to compare his grief?
Job 6:1-3

2.)   How does Job describe his situation?
Job 6:4-7

3.)   What is Job's wish?
Job 6:8-13

4.)   What does Job have to say about his friends?

Job 6:14-21

5.)   To continue his thought Job asks his friends questions in relation to his calamity.
       What are they and what point is he trying to make?

Job 6:22-24

6.)   How does Job view his friends' words towards him?

Job 6:25-30

7.)   What torment is Job suffering?

Job 7:1-10

8.)   What is it that Job will not do?

Job 7:11

9.)   What is Job's desire?

Job 7:12-16

10.)   Job ends his speech frustrated. What does he say and how would he prefer it to end?

Job 7:17-21

PERSONAL QUESTIONS

A.)   What response would you have if your family member or friends came to you in a similar fashion as Eliphaz did in his previous chapter?

B.)   Can you receive help from someone who is not going through the same situation or problem you're facing? Explain.

C.)   People love to give visions to one another and dreams. How do you believe most people accept them? Is there a time and place for prophetic dreams?

Reference – Genesis 37:1-10, 1 Samuel 3:1-18

JUST A THOUGHT

Just a reminder, most of Job is a poetic and uses a lot of metaphor. Instead of saying, "I'm sad", the characters might compare their sadness to a mother bird missing her chicks or a stream over-flowing a dam. Think about the imagery that is being used not only from this lesson but for future ones as well. There are many metaphors used in this book, please do not skip them while speed-reading. Instead, let it marinate and ask God for direction in figuring out what is being said and implied.

For example Job compares his friends to a stream in the middle of a desert (Job 6:14-21). This means that while the rain is flowing then they're available as a natural resource for help. However, during an extreme summer they dry up and are no longer available. Once you stop and realize what is being said, many of us can identify with Job. We all know people who are in your life during good times, but, once life get strenuous then they're nowhere to be found.

Using a stream in the desert is just one example of metaphors used in the book of Job, which will be helpful in allowing you to connect to its message. There are plethora of knowledge and wisdom within this book, but it's given in a poetic package of metaphors and examples. Don't by pass them but study to find out how deep and awe inspiring the message can teach.

To Those Who Forget God

Lesson 5

Job 8

1.)   How does Bildad start his response to Job?
Job 8:1-3

2.)   Remembering how Job's children are depicted in chapter 1, what does Bildad say in regards to their situation?
Job 8:4

3.)   What does Bildad say to encourage Job?
Job 8:5-7

4.)   Who does Bildad suggest Job to search and why?

Job 8:8-10

5.)   In verse 13 Bildad talks about those who forget God. Describe what he believes will happen to them.

Job 8:11-19

6.)   What does Bildad have to say about God and His actions?

Job 8:20-22

PERSONAL QUESTIONS

A.)   If Bildad came to you and you're going through the misery of Job, how would you respond to his encouragement and explain?

B.)   There is an association made between Job's children behavior and the punishment they received. If a person came up to you and stated the exact same thing about your family members or friends how would you respond?

C.)   What can make a person forget about God being in their lives?

JUST A THOUGHT

Bildad was the second friend of Job to respond in this book. Unlike Eliphaz who started his statement with a compliment, Bildad immediately attacked Job. He even said some words about Job's children, which was bold, but I assume Bildad thought it was okay because they're friends. Bildad was a Shuhite who are descendants of Abraham's youngest son Shuah from Keturah (Genesis 25:1-6). There's not much more about Shuah except that his brother was Midian. It is from Midian we know that he eventually settled East with many of his brethren and started a place where Moses eventually lived in exile. Because of Midian's family close connection to Shuah, it's very possible that the story of Job became an oral tradition in that area.

Justice

Lesson 6

Job 9-10

1.)   Job lists many attributes about God and His power. Read the following verses and list at least three of them.

Job 9:1-10

2.)   Often, we like to believe that people can contend with God using words. What does Job say about the results of doing this?

Job 9:11-16

3.)   While being down, what does Job say about how God treats him?

Job 9:17-19

4.)   In the previous chapter, Bildad gave his description of God dealing with the wicked

         and righteous. What does Job say regarding the same subject?

Job 9:20-24

5.)   What metaphor does Job give regarding his days?

Job 9:25-26

6.)   What does Job believe he need regarding his situation and why?

Job 9:27-35

7.)   In the midst of his complaint, Job began to ask a series of questions to God. What are they and why is he doing this?

Job 10:1-7

8.)   How does Job describe his coming into being?

Job 10:8-13

9.)   Job often talks about innocence and wickedness. In the text Job 10:14-17, how does Job feel about his own innocence or guilty feelings and God's response to them? Explain why you believe Job felt this way.

10.)   To end his speech what did Job say? How is this similar to previous declarations? Job 10:18-22

PERSONAL QUESTIONS

A.)   Justice is a common thought that permeates through the talks of Job and his friends. What is the main difference between Job and his friends view on justice from God towards people?

B.)   Do you feel like there is justice in our world, country, and community?

JUST A THOUGHT

There is a strong case for justice that is being made by Job in contrast with Bildad and Eliphaz. The idea is that he wants to know if a person can truly have justice. The word that is used in verse 2 of chapter 9 is Tsadeq. In Hebrew, it relates to *"righteousness, being acquitted, or even being declared right"*. To Job it's tough and actually almost impossible to get justice because you're dealing with an all-powerful Being. For Eliphaz and Bildad God is fair for the righteous and punishes the wicked.

Look at how Job regards getting justice compare to his friends. Often a person's mindset is changed depending on their situation. In Job's case, he is the one going through the suffering compare to his three friends who are outside of the situation.

In our lives, we can view justice differently depending on our situation and problems. For example if you're on trial for a crime that you didn't committed and the jury are against you, then your view of the justice system is different compare to your friends who are looking at your case as an outsider.

Zophar's Appeal

Lesson 7

Job 11

1.)   How did Zophar start his response to Job? Why do you think he began this way?

Job 11:1-3

2.)   What comment of Job's did Zophar use to rebuke?

Job 11:4

3.)   What is Zophar's wish that God will do for Job?

Job 11:5-6

4.)   Why is it not possible to learn of God's power and secrets?

Job 11:7-10

5.)   Whom does God know?

Job 11:11-12

6.)   Zophar encourages Job to have a better disposition and remove sin from his life. List what Zophar says that would help.

Job 11:13-17

7.)   Hope is described in the last part of the chapter for two groups of people. The righteous and the wicked. Describe each group in the context of the scripture.

Job 11:18-20

PERSONAL QUESTIONS

A.)   Much like Eliphaz and Bildad, Zophar wanted to encourage Job. Look over what he said and put yourself in Job's place. How would you respond to Zophar's appeal?

B.)   The text talks about safety in hope. Why is this true? What things do you hope for in your life?

C.)   Zophar accuses Job of doing something wrong and implores him to repent. Job believes he's innocent. What would you say to someone who is asking you to repent for an act that you know you didn't do?

D.)   There is a part in Job 11:6-10, that talks about how hard it is to have a complete understanding of God. Why is this true, and would God want to reveal everything to us? Could that be helpful or harmful for us to know everything about God?

JUST A THOUGHT

Unlike the other two men, Zophar's family group Naamathite is a little harder to trace in the Bible. There are several cases of people named Naamah but this would have came hundreds of years after Job. There is a family of Naamites listed in Numbers 26:40-41 that are related to the tribe of Benjamin, which is a different group but similar name. It is believed that Naamah was a city in Canaan but nothing more is really said regarding Zophar's heritage. The safe assumption is that he has a similar standing with Eliphaz and Bildad. However, as you will see, Zophar is only mentioned to speak once more in the book of Job. Bildad and Eliphaz both speak at least three different times to Job. There is another possible time Zophar's speaks but that will be revealed when we get to that lesson.

Job's Response

Lesson 8

Job 12-13:12

1.)   What is Job's response?

Job 12:1-5

2.)   What flourishes in Job's opinion?

Job 12:6

3.)   Who teaches us about God?

Job 12:7-12

4.)   What does Job say about wisdom?

Job 12:13

5.)   List Job's examples of God's power.

Job 12:14-16

6.)   Regarding people with power, list the various acts that show God is in control of
        them.

Job 12:17-25

7.)   What does Job want to do?

Job 13:1-3

8.)   What does Job call his friends and wishes from them?

Job 13:4-5

9.)   What idea does Job present to his friends on how they represent God?

Job 13:6-12

PERSONAL QUESTIONS

A.)   What are ways that we can represent God?

B.)   Job informs his friends on how their words are misrepresenting God. Is it possible for the church as a whole and as an individual to misrepresent God? Explain your answer for both.

C.)　　Job's view on God's power is filtered through the calamity he is suffering. How can a bad situation affect our view of God's interaction in our lives?

D.)　　Have you ever had a situation where you blamed God during a bad time in your life? What was it and how did you overcome having such a negative view of God?

JUST A THOUGHT

Job lashes out at his friends because they assume he was guilty. In Job's mind, he has done nothing to receive such harsh punishment. Because his friends state they're representing God, this also makes Job go against the Almighty as well.

We often lash out against people who we feel as a threat. This is basic survival and Job was doing it as well against his friends. He felt terrible and the words of his friends were not helping the situation. To Job it only made things worst.

Not only this lesson, but for future lessons as well, put yourself in Job and his friend's place. What if you were going through a horrific pain or terrible situation that was no fault of you own? What if you had a friend or family member who was going through a situation that appeared to be self-inflicted?

Remember Job chapters 1-2 and who really caused pain in Job's life. Sometimes outside factors happen to teach a lesson for everyone willing to learn from that person overcoming the trial.

Though He Slay Me

Lesson 9

Job 13:13-14

1.)   What does Job tell his friends?

Job 13:13

2.)   What does Job declare?

Job 13:14-19

3.)   Job requests two things, what are they?

Job 13:20-21

4.)   What are some questions Job has for God? How does he feel like he's being treated
        by the Almighty?

Job 13:22-25

5.)   Read Job 14:1-6. What is Job describing?

6.)   What knowledge is Job sharing regarding trees and plants?

Job 14:7-9

7.)   How does Job view death?

Job 14:10-12

8.)   What is Job's wish from God?

Job 14:13-22

PERSONAL QUESTIONS

A.)   Describe the difference between plants and animals in what we perceive as birth, life, and death.

B.)   What view do you have regarding your own life? Is it full of sin, perfect, or a mix? Explain.

C.)   If you had to defend yourself, what would you say to God? What examples could you
use to defend yourself?

JUST A THOUGHT

The title of this Bible Study comes from Job 13:15. It simply reads, "Though He slay me, yet will I trust Him: but I will maintain mine own ways before Him." In context, this line comes from Job when he is transitioning from arguing with his friends to taking his case to the Lord. He recognizes that his friends are displaying a false example of God (Job 13:7-10), and decides to make himself known to the Almighty for justice. Job isn't delusional. He understands the difference between mortal man and an all-powerful God. He knows that even in the best-case scenario he's no match for God but is determined to let it be known that he is innocent of any wrongdoing that would have caused his current situation.

The interesting thing is that out of context, this verse (Job 13:15) sounds like that no matter what is going on, I will trust the Lord. Which is true but not quite what Job is intending. Remember that they are in full belief that God blesses the righteous and punishes the wicked. Therefore, to Job, his suffering could be attributed to God, and is making it clear that he is innocent.

Another interesting fact is how various translations can differ slightly with this text. Go to various sites or down load a Bible app that has different versions and see how they're different. For example, the New King James Version (NKJV), New International Version (NIV), and English Standard Version (ESV) all have a similar message to the King James Version (KJV). However, the Contemporary English Bible (CEB) and World English Bible (WEB) talk about having no hope after it speaks about God slaying him. In the Good News Bible (GNB), Job lost his hope so what if God kills him.

Different versions are an example of what happens when people go back and try to interpret what was being said. There are nuances in the text that will make each version a little different depending on how you read accent marks and vowels from the original language. In Hebrew, there are plethoras of marks that can change words or emphasis on words. This will sometimes change the wording of a Biblical passage from one version to the next.

The best-case scenario is to get a version that you like and trust. Talk with a minister and go to the scripture in the Bible that you like or read often. Then compare this scripture in various versions. Study and pray to receive what is the version God is leading you to use as your primary source. However, do not discount other versions. Often scriptures have been cleared due to more knowledge or studying the Bible with an objective mindset.

The Ways of Evil

Lesson 10

Job 15

1.)   Eliphaz responds to Job. His first statement is a few questions to begin his argument. What are they and why would he say this?

Job 15:1-3

2.)   What does Eliphaz have to say about Job's words are doing to him?

Job 15:4-6

3.)   Eliphaz tries to bring Job down and humble him. Describe what he says.

Job 15:7-16

4.)   Where is Eliphaz getting his ideas?

Job 15:17-19

5.)   Describe the days and actions of the wicked/evil in the mindset of Eliphaz.

Job 15:20-28

6.)   List some of the issues/problems that will come to the wicked.

Job 15:29-35

PERSONAL QUESTIONS

A.)   Eliphaz, like Bildad and Zophar, are obsessed with the evil and wicked being punished. Why do you believe they are sticking to this point in regards to the eventual end of the wicked?

B.)   There are several lists regarding wicked behavior. Read some of the scriptures and write what you notice about the actions and behavior listed. Are there personal issues in the list?

Romans 1:18-32, Galatians 5:19-21, Proverbs 6:16-19, Ezekiel 16:48-50

C.)   If you were able to declare things that are evil, what acts and behaviors would go on that list? Why do you believe you chose these specific acts?

D.)   Is it possible for a person to be fully righteous and wicked? Explain.

JUST A THOUGHT

If you were to mix grape and apple juices into the same glass, the new mix would be a blend. It wouldn't be fully either but a new mix containing both. This would make the new drink something different. It's a blend of both juices for a new flavor.

When we try to be both good and bad, we are now an amalgamation of both characteristics. No one can be purely good but we should at least try to be 100% of what God wants us to be. It's not easy, but imagine if you were to separate the contents of both juices. It would take heat and various straining capabilities to start with the original two juices.

This is the same with us if we are to be truly removed from sin and evil. If God were to remove sin from our lives, the process is tough and strenuous. However, He has a plan and desires for everyone to walk in the path set by God. Instead of mulling around with bad, evil, or wicked ideas and actions, try your best to stay pure in what God wants you to be.

If You Were in My Situation

Lesson 11

Job 16-17

1.)   What is Job's initial response to Eliphaz?

Job 16:1-3

2.)   Job compares himself to his friends if the situation was reverse. List some of the
       things Job would say or do to them if they had lost everything.

Job 16:4-6

3.)   Job began to find fault in what God has allowed or done. Even though he is
        talking to his friends, why does Job send his complaint to God?

Job 16:7-8

4.)   Describe some of the things Job's enemies have done to him.

Job 16:9-10

5.)   Who has Job been turned over too, and what metaphor does he use to describe his
        pain?

Job 16:11-14

6.)   How has Job react to the situation?

Job 16:15-17

7.)   What is it that Job desires? What does he want in Heaven before God?

Job 16:18-22

8.)   Describe Job's poetic lamentations or complaint about his situation.

Job 17:1-7

9.)   What is it that Job will not find amongst his friends?

Job 17:8-10

10.)   What is Job's complaint at the end of his response?

Job 17:11-16

PERSONAL QUESTIONS

A.)   Job was upset with his friends because he believed they were not there for him. What purpose do you believe friends serve in our lives?

B.)   Imagine one of your family members or friends going through a serious calamity (untreatable sickness, family problems, financial horrors, crime committed against them). If you were in their life and going through their struggle, what would you want to hear to be encouraged?

C.)   How do you give hope to someone who believes there is no way out of a terrible situation?

JUST A THOUGHT

It's interesting to note that nowhere in the Book of Job does our main character send for his friends to come. I'm sure there were some correspondence and for a person of power and wealth to go through the pain that he went through, the news had to reach everyone. Imagine right now the most powerful or richest person in your community, state, or country. If they went through a plethora of horrors like losing their children, going bankrupt, and getting a painful disease at the same time surely that news would permeate through society.

However, Job's friends came of their own accord and now in Job's eyes they're not acting friendly. He would probably rather someone to encourage him and be on his side then to condemn. Think about your family and friends. Whom is someone that you feel comfortable speaking with no matter the issue? There are probably people right now that you do not want to share because instead of being helpful and encouraging they will only tear you down and chastise. Now think of yourself. Are you a person that others want to speak with or would avoid?

The Wicked Will Fail

Lesson 12

Job 18

1.)   Bildad responds to Job's remarks. How does Bildad defend himself and Job's
       friends?

Job 18:1-4

2.)   Next to each scripture listed, describe what will happen to wicked/evil people.

Job 18:5-6

:7-8

continue on next page

:9-10

:11-13

:14-15

:16-17

3.)   What is Bildad's conclusion for the wicked?
Job 18:18-21

PERSONAL QUESTIONS

A.)   Why would Bildad believe that wicked people would get the results he lists in this chapter?

B.)   Do you agree with Bildad's conclusion on what will happen to wicked people?

C.)   Is Bildad's words in this chapter encouraging for someone who is in the midst of suffering?

JUST A THOUGHT

Bildad list a long stream of consequences for wicked and evil people. Their eventual end will be in destruction and he wanted to make sure Job knew that. It is clear in Bildad's mind the ultimate end for whom he believes are wicked. Although he might come across as a person who is a bit harsh, we currently have the same mindset.

In the book of Revelations and many gospels, there are comments about the eventual end to wickedness. There are even stories and mythos about Hell and what will eventually happen to all those who will not obey God. There were at time when ministers in the 1940's through the 1960's were known as Fire and Brimstone pastors. Many people believe that idea is true now, but do our lives reflect this? There are of course cases where a person does self-harm or something to people and they are either punished or sick from that choice. However, there are many times when someone might cheat or gain wealth through nefarious ways. If they go unpunished, other people will not only fail to condemn them but might mold their own behavior after these people. For example if someone is a jerk and their crass behavior gets them a better position, other people follow suit and become jerks.

Think for yourself on what is good and bad behavior. The most important thing is to compare God's standard to what you see around you. What might be right for one person could be wrong for another. If in doubt, go with what God is informing you to do.

For example, a cactus and a water lily are both plants. However, both species need completely different environments to thrive. The cactus can live in extreme heat and dry land. The water lily needs a pond or some large body of water. Both are plants but each has adapted to an environment where they can thrive.

What is your environment? Where does God want you so you can thrive?

When All Are Against You...
Still Have Joy

Lesson 13

Job 19

1.)   What is Job's immediate response to Bildad?
Job 19:1-6

2.)   List the actions that Job feels God has done to him.
Job 19:7-12

3.)   Describe the treatment to Job by his friends and visitors.

Job 19:13-14

4.)   What does Job's workers/employees think of Job and treats him?

Job 19:15-16

5.)   How does Job's wife and young people view him?

Job 19:17-18

6.)   What treatment does he receive from his close friends?

Job 19:19

7.)   What is he requesting from his friends?

Job 19:20-22

8.)   What does Job wish could happen?

Job 19:23-24

9.)   What hope and knowledge does Job have?

Job 19:25-27

10.)   What warning does Job give to his friends?

Job 19:28-29

PERSONAL QUESTIONS

A.)   Jesus is the ultimate redeemer. However, a redeemer is someone who helps someone on trial or going through a tough situation. This means that a lawyer or anyone can actually redeem or stand in for someone else. Why is it important for us to have a redeemer in our lives and are there moments that you can be a redeemer for someone else?

B.)   In spite of his afflictions, Job still had hope about being redeemed. Can you think of a moment when you had joy and hope in spite of the problems in your life, what was it and write it down? Remember that moment when things get hard to bring joy in your life.

C.)   Why is it important to have faith in God during tough times? What does this reveal about your relationship with Him?

D.)   List people or situations that hinder your ministry for God. Then pray and "X" them out as a way of showing, that with God it will no longer be a problem for you.

JUST A THOUGHT

It's easy to have joy when times are awesome and blessings are overflowing. Everyone talks about how great it is when the Lord blesses them. Especially when you have a newborn child, new car, job promotion, or anything else that brings joy to your life. It takes a real relationship with God to have joy in the midst of problems. To see or be happy during those moments is not only tough but reveals the strength of your relationship in Jesus.

For example, think about a relationship or friendship. It's easy to be familiar and enjoy yourself when life is going well. However, allow something tragic or tough to happen and see who you're drawn too. Who is the person or people that when life gets hard you want them in you corner? Those are the people that you have a true relationship with and will be there when times are good and bad situation.

The Destruction of the Wicked

Lesson 14

Job 20

1.)   Why does Zophar feel compel to speak?
Job 20:1-3

2.)   According to Zophar what will ultimately happen to those who are wicked?
Job 20:4-5

3.)   List a few tragic events that will happen to bad people.
Job 20:9-11

4.)   What metaphor does Zophar uses to give an example of partaking wicked behavior?

Job 20:12-18

5.)   What are some of the actions people deep in wickedness are willing to do?

Job 20:19-22

6.)   Zophar suggests how they should be handled by God. What is it?

Job 20:23

7.)   In the end what will happen to a wicked person and their things?

Job 20:24-29

PERSONAL QUESTIONS

A.)   How is Zophar views similar to Bildad?

B.)   Zophar is compelled to speak. What is something that compels you to action? Think of something that will make you want to do something great.

C.)   What are some of the affects you see from people who are considered evil or wicked? How are they affecting you personally and in your community as well?

JUST A THOUGHT

At the beginning of his speech, Zophar talks about how he is compelled to talk. He's stating this because of the conversation that is going on and of course, he feels like he's being attacked by Job. This made him want to say something to defend himself and to correct Job.

Zophar feels like he has to say something and often times we go through periods in our lives when we are called to action. Often we want to say something to people to correct them or change their behavior. Other moments we actually feel compel to do something great, help people, or create something new. Whatever motivates you, use it to make yourself, family, and community better. Sometimes it can be through talking with someone, singing, creating a new invention, or showing kindness to all you meet.

Lifestyle of the Wicked and Sinful

Lesson 15

Job 21

1.)   Job responded to his friends and wanted to grab their attention. What does Job say
       and why do you think he started this way?

Job 21:1-6

2.)   What does Job say regarding the wicked?

Job 21:7-9

3.)   What examples are given to reveal the success of the wicked/sinners?

Job 21:10-13

4.)   What does the sinner say to God and why?

Job 21:14-16

5.)   What does Job wish could happened to bad people?

Job 21:17-21

6.)   Describe the two people Job gives for example. What is their ultimate fate?

Job 21:22-26

7.)   Job continues his speech by asking some questions he's assuming his friends will

        say. What are they and his answer to them?

Job 21:27-33

8.)   Ultimately what does Job say about his friends' response?

Job 21:34

PERSONAL QUESTIONS

A.)   In this ongoing battle regarding the wicked and their behavior, why would Job take the stance found in this chapter?

B.)   Does Job viewpoint represent the current world we live in?

C.)   What is your view on the wicked/evil/un-repented sinner of this world? Do you believe they get what they deserve?

JUST A THOUGHT

In chapter 21 verses 7 through 14, Job gives a realistic view of the wicked. In reality, he's talking about people in general. There are segments of the population who live, thrive, and then die. They have no desire to learn about God and build a relationship with Him. They would prefer to live without God and some have even ushered in an era to remove Him from our lives. As you can see, not everyone who hates, distrust, or doesn't believe in God is the poorest, struggling, or diseased people on the Earth. On the contrary, many people are thriving financially without a belief in God. They want to live their lives and then die.

Although Job was referring to his time, even now we are going through a similar situation. Think about some of the people you see on the news, TV, movies, or on the web. There are hundreds if not thousands of people who are thriving. The end is still the same. Death. And death without God is something that most of us would never want to consider or desire.

The idea is that happiness is not found in your wealth. If you measure happiness like that, then your instruments are wrong. In reality, peace comes from God. In addition, there is knowledge in Him, of something great in this life and after. I'm not here to sell you a pipe dream or live in a fantasy. Think about how God wants the best for you now and after His soon return.

Joy is measured in your loving relationship with God and people. So I do not want you to feel like being poor is the "it" thing to guarantee safe passage into Heaven. Many poor people do not have a relationship with God and plenty of wealthy people love the Lord. Instead, just trust God and seek the ways He has for you. Now and in the future, you will be filled with joy because of that decision.

Following God Almighty

Lesson 16

Job 22

1.)	Eliphaz responds to Job first by asking a series of questions. What are they and what point is he trying to prove?

Job 22:1-5

2.)	What does Eliphaz have to say about those who are privilege and have wealth?

Job 22:6-11

3.)   According to Eliphaz, where is God?

Job 22:12

4.)   Why do we believe God cannot be a part of our lives? What reason/excuse does
       Eliphaz give from people?

Job 22:13-16

5.)   What is the difference in mindset between sinners and righteous?

Job 22:17-20

6.)   What does Eliphaz suggest for Job to do? What would Job receive from this counsel?
Job 22:21-23

7.)   What blessings does Eliphaz mention after being with God Almighty?
Job 22:24-25

8.)   What are some advantages to following God?
Job 22:26-30

PERSONAL QUESTIONS

A.)   In your life when does God show you favor?

B.)   Do you believe there is a difference in mindset between the righteous and wicked? Explain your answer.

C.)   Can people behavior and mindset always be the same or are there times when it's different?

D.)   Why is it a good thing to follow God? Are there benefits?

JUST A THOUGHT

This chapter, like many of Job's friends, starts with them either defending themselves or chastising Job. Eliphaz does something, which is quite interesting, a little later in his speech in regards to Job's situation.

Eliphaz begins with a rebuke of Job. In the past, he talked to Job more in the general sense of wickedness but now he was blaming or accusing Job of various acts. He wanted to make sure that Job knew of his bad behavior and the source of his ills and bad fortune. That goes into the second part of Eliphaz's speech which relates to how wicked people will be punished, which is the common motif in this book. Another familiar idea is that God will punish the wicked. Job is being punished therefore he must be wicked. In the end, he has suggestions for Job to change his ways so the punishment will stop.

In verse 24, we learn about the town of Ophir. According to various scholars, this city was known for its gold and people would often have trades and dealings with them. Eliphaz uses this city as an example for Job to forgo his possessions and gold, and take on God as his treasure. At first, this sounds like a common thought that we have to lay aside your earthly possessions and take on spiritual ones. The problem is that Job had already lost his earthly possessions and his health is bad as well. As far as giving up stuff, it was taken from him.

This means that either Eliphaz was talking of a spiritual and mental mindset of giving up things or he was disconnected from reality of Job's current situation and possibly assumed Job had more possessions. Don't let your pride or self worth get in the way but turn to God. Of course, if that were true, why would Job willingly be in a mess if he had access to help him out of his current situation?

This talk from Eliphaz is a great example of when people are caught up in their speech or idea to the point that they lose focus on the reality around them. Sometimes we might suggest to someone to do something and that person has either already failed at that task or they do not have the means to complete what you're suggesting. Make sure that when offering help or advice to someone; first take it up with God. Make sure He's the one who is in control and not you saying something out of personal reason or spite.

Problem in this World

Lesson 17

Job 23-24

1.)   What is it that Job wishes?

Job 23:1-5

2.)   How does Job believe God will respond?

Job 23:6-9

3.)   Why does Job feel he will come out of his current plight?

Job 23:10-12

4.)   In spite of confidence, how does Job feel towards God's action and power in his life?

Job 23:13-17

5.)   What question does Job want answered?

Job 24:1

6.)   Describe some of the issues in the world. Do you see some of the same problems currently?

Job 24:2-11

7.)   Look at the answers from the previous question, how do people respond to these problems and what is God's response?

Job 24:12

8.)   List some of the actions wicked people do against others.

Job 24:13-22

9.)   How will it end for wicked people? How does Job feel about this?

Job 24:23-25

PERSONAL QUESTIONS

A.)   Look at question 9. Are there similarities between what Job and his friends said regarding the wicked?

B.)   What problems do you see in this world? Make a list for worldwide, local, and in your home.

C.)   Do problems or issues change a person's mindset and/or behavior? Please explain.

D.)   Look at your life. Has there been a time when a circumstance changed your view on an issue or something in your life?

JUST A THOUGHT

Job offers a rebuttal as usual to Eliphaz's comments. I'm quite sure he was able to look at his situation and question some of what his friend had to say regarding his lifestyle. The calamites that happened to him took everything and Job was a living testimony to that fact. He brings on two very interesting points in a speech full of proclamations and metaphors.

The first is found in chapter 23 when Job has a desire to talk with God. He wants to argue his case before the Lord. Unlike previous times, he doesn't set out for an intermediary or someone to speak on his behalf. Now Job believes he can do this by himself. Some of this was probably him arguing with his friends and in his mind winning the arguments. He felt like if they were a representative of God, and he was debating with them, certainly he could do the same with God. After all, God will have to take notice of his arguments as to why he is innocent of receiving such harsh punishment.

Sometimes we have a similar mindset. There are people who believe they can philosophically battle with God or even question the mere thought of His existence. They believe that by debating or arguing with those who represent the Lord, means that they could debate or battle God in a similar fashion. Even people in the church, with behavior and words believe they can impose their will over God's. It sounds strange but we do it all the time when we either assume God will or won't do something in your life without consulting Him, or simply do what you feel like and figure the Lord will understand.

The second thought that Job had was regarding the suffering of the world. To him the poor and weak suffer while the wicked and wealthy thrive. God is nowhere to be seen to help those or set up vindication. To him the bad people are doing great and the Lord's justice is not around.

Many people have this idea in our current timeframe as well. We believe there is no justice when bad people seem to thrive and good people suffer and die. Just like in Job, this is often an oversimplification of the world. We forget that sin and evil is present across the globe. Bad things happen daily. Also in regards to the wicked or evil people, many of them suffer. Sometimes from self-inflicted wounds due to addictions, being imprisoned, or even executed depending on how heinous of an act they committed. In regards to the poor, many people and organizations are out there helping and trying to make a difference.

In reality, many people complain about the world they're living in but have no desire to change it for the better. You can have multitude of videos and shows about wanting to give to charities or volunteering at various functions to help your city. A few people will watch or care or even show up to help. Have something that does nothing for the community and is destructive on a personal and community level, then everyone participates if it looks fun. We can't complain about what's going on if you're not going to be a part of the solution to help.

Retribution Will Come

Lesson 18

Job 25-27

1.)   What is Bildad's response to Job?

Job 25:1-6

2.)   In response to Bildad, Job lists a few questions. What are they and why do you think he started his retort this way?

Job 26:1-4

3.)   What is being said in regards to the dead?

Job 26:5-6

4.)   What symbols and examples are used to explain God's power?

Job 26:7-14

5.)   What is something that Job will not do?

Job 27:1-4

6.)   To his friends what is something Job will never admit and why?

Job 27:5-6

7.)   What is the desire for his enemies to be handled?

Job 27:7-10

8.)   What will be taught to those willing to listen?

Job 27:11-12

9.)   Write below a few things that will happen to the wicked.

Job 27:13-23

PERSONAL QUESTIONS

A.)   Is there justice in God's system?

B.)   When you think about the difference between God and humans, why would an all-powerful Being risk it all to save us?

JUST A THOUGHT

These groups of chapters are actually quite interesting. Not just because of what's being said. Many of the speeches here mirror that of what was being talked about God, suffering, the righteous, wickedness, and so forth. Instead according to scholars and religious texts specialist there could be more then the two people talking within chapters 25-27.

It's clear that Bildad starts his speech in chapter 25. It is unusually short compare to all previous speeches. Many people have attributed chapter 26 verses 5 through 14 as also being Bildad. For some reason, there was a break or Job came in at the beginning of 26 and Bildad finished his thought. Also, there is no Zophar. He does not get a third speech like Eliphaz and Bildad. This has lead to people believing that Zophar's speech is amalgamation shown in chapter 27 verses 7 through 23 or even starting at verse 13.

When reading the Bible most versions will have chapters 26 and 27 attributed to Job. There's no clear break so the assumption is that he spoke the entirety of both. However, there are some versions of the Bible that shows different people speaking in brackets. Others just put huge spaces in between the thoughts.

As of now look at it as though there is talk regarding the various issues that have been stated already. Apply it to your life as though they are talking to you and you're able to see what is going on. It could be Job is bringing up a variety of points or that there is more of a conversation-taking place. Regardless learn what you can from this group of scriptures and pray to find out what God wants you to learn.

For more information, please check the Bibliography as a good starting point to find more information.

The Importance of Wisdom

Lesson 19

Job 28

1.)   Describe the poetic metaphor Job uses to start this chapter.

Job 28:1-11

2.)   After the metaphor what is Job's referring too?

Job 28:12-13

3.)   Where are some of the places, you can't find, what Job is talking about?

Job 28:14-16

4.)   What are some of the items, you can't compare to the answer in question 2?
Job 28:17-19

5.)   What is Job's question? Why do you believe he was asking?
Job 28:20-22

6.)   Who understands Job's subject? What examples does he use?
Job 28:23-26

7.)   How do you obtain wisdom?
Job 28:27-28

PERSONAL QUESTIONS

A.)   Why is wisdom important to obtain?

B.)   If given wisdom equal to Solomon's, what decision would you make? How would you change your life, family, community?

JUST A THOUGHT

Before going into his final statement, Job has a discourse about wisdom, which is an idea that is invaluable to all people. It allows us to make the best decision regardless of the situation. Solomon is considered the wisest man to live. He asked for wisdom to help him rule God's people.

Many books of the Bible are referred to as wisdom books. They are Ecclesiastes, Song of Solomon, Lamentations, Proverbs, Psalm, and Job. Inside these books is a wealth of knowledge. They're told in a variety of ways to explain or show metaphors in having wisdom for various daily issues.

When thinking about asking for stuff from God, and we all do. Start with wisdom. After all what are riches if you don't have any knowledge of how to spend or use the resource. What good is health if you're not wise to keep great care of your body? Why have random knowledge if you're not going to put it to great practical and spiritual use.

If you truly want to make a difference in your life and those you touch, ask for wisdom. Allow a changed and growing mindset to happen. You want wisdom so you can best manage your life through these hard times and are able to become an example for others in how to live.

Job's Final Statement

Lesson 20

Job 29-31

1.)   What does Job desire?

Job 29:1-6

2.)   Next to the verse, write something that Job is referring to from his past.

Job 29:7-10

Continue on next page

:11-17

:18-20

:21-25

3.)   What does Job have to say about the young? How are they treated in the
        community?

Job 30:1-8

4.)   How does Job feel like he's being treated? What examples does he give?
Job 30:9-15

5.)   Describe Job's suffering.
Job 30:16-23

6.)   Describe Job's agony. How do you think this would affect his mental state?
Job 30:24-31

7.)   In chapter 31 Job ends his defense to vindicate his mindset and situation. How does he begin?

Job 31:1-4

8.)   What is the next issue? If anything is wrong, what is Job willing to do?

Job 31:5-8

9.)   How does Job feel about the next sin he's is referring? If he's guilty what is the inevitable outcome?

Job 31:9-12

10.)   What is the next dilemma?

Job 31:13-15

11.)   What are some of the charitable things Job believes should happen and if not then
        what should happen to him?

Job 31:16-23

12.)   What is Job stating we should not put our trust in and why?

Job 31:24-28

13.)   How does Job view treating others/strangers/enemies?

Job 31:29-32

14.)   What is another sin he mentions and whom does he compare it too?

Job 31:33-34

15.)   What is Job willing to do for the Lord?

Job 31:35-37

16.)   What is Job's final statement regarding his problem?

Job 31:38-40

PERSONAL QUESTIONS

A.)   Why would Job end his final statement the way he did?

JUST A THOUGHT

This is a long lesson that covers the end of Job's statement. After this, we will get a new person who will talk for several chapters and God will make his own proclamations about Himself. It's here that we learn a variety of things from Job but there are a few basic ideas as well.

Job remembers his past when life was grand. For Job, it wasn't about money but his positive affect on people. How great it was to be a blessing to others. There are various times when Job remembers how he would do something for all people, regardless of wealth, class, or status.

There is a great lesson to be learned from here. It's not that you're wealthy or have money. Life is more about how you are treating others and affecting people in a positive manner.

Then Job looked at himself being treated in the community. He goes into a long speech about society's treatment and his life. He understands it's a different view compare to when he was rich and powerful.

We do that as well, look over our lives, and see how people are treating us. It's often easy to recall when we're treated bad or if someone is out to get us. Those situations are easy to remember. The times when people are still nice and treat you kind sometimes go unnoticed. In Job's case that was possible, but for him, he was going through a hard trial. All he could see was how awful people regarded him and treated his life.

The last thing was Job's idea to offer retribution for anything that could have been the cause of his calamity. There's a list as you just read regarding various issues and heartaches that if he has caused he's more than willing to help.

The amazing thing here is that Job is even thinking of others at a time like this. He wasn't sure if his pain was caused by bad behavior or wickedness and figured to make atonement for anyone who was harmed by him. Job's idea was to make things right for people so he can proceed with a better life.

Thinking of others and reflecting on your past in hard times is tough. However, it reveals that it's not impossible. It's easy to remember when people have treated us wrong. Tougher to turn it around; think about that when praying to God. Think about those moments if you've harmed or did anything to someone else. Is there someone you need to say sorry or pray for because of a past behavior? Try putting others, even during bad times, before yourself. It's a great lesson to learn and remember God's character growing in you.

The Start of Elihu's Appeal

Lesson 21

Job 32-33

1.)   Why did Job's friends stop responding?

Job 32:1

2.)   Who is Elihu and how did he feel about Job and the three men?

Job 32:2-5

3.)   How does Elihu begin his statement? Why did he wait before responding?

Job 32:6-13

4.)   Why does Elihu feel justified to respond to everyone?

Job 32:14-22

5.)   How does Elihu start his opening statement?

Job 33:1-7

6.)   What statement does Elihu used from Job to continue his argument?

Job 33:8-11

7.)   How does Elihu respond to Job's statement?

Job 33:12-13

8.)   According to Elihu, how does God communicate? What examples does he give?

Job 33:14-17

9.)   What actions will God use toward people and why?

Job 33:18-21

10.)   What does Elihu state about God when people approach the proverbial pit?
Job 33:22-24

11.)   What happened when a righteous person is before the Lord?
Job 33:25-28

12.)   What is Elihu plan for Job?
Job 33:29-33

PERSONAL QUESTIONS

A.)   Elihu being a younger man wants his turn to chastise and correct Job, what does this say about respect from younger people, and how should that be exhibited now?

B.)   Why do you believe Elihu pleas with Job to listen to him?

C.)   What lesson can you teach other people? Are there experiences that you have gone through that might be useful to others?

JUST A THOUGHT

In this chapter, we're introduced to another of Job's friends. It's a little strange because he was not mentioned with the other three at the beginning of the book (chapter 2:11). Either he came a little later or due to him being a youth, was not mentioned in the beginning. However, Elihu heard the conversation and knew what was going on with Job and the three men arguments against him.

Elihu goes for six chapters, which will give us a chance to learn more about him and what he has to say. The interesting thing is that the Bible states how he is wrathful or angry with Job and the three men. He believes that Job is self-righteous, and can stand against God, when it comes to judgment. With the three men, Elihu is angry with them for not revealing God in a great light and making Him look guilty compare to Job.

Elihu was from the Buzites who have their linage through Buz the son of Nahor, who was Abraham's brother (Genesis 22:20-21). Nahor got his name from his grandfather who had Terah. For more information on the genealogy of Nahor and Abraham, read Genesis 11:10-26. It starts with Shem and continues in detail regarding the various people in Abraham's family line.

Difference Between God and Men

Lesson 22

Job 34-35

1.)   What metaphor does Elihu use for listening?

Job 34:1-4

2.)   What statement did Elihu repeat of Job's?

Job 34:5-6

3.)   How does Elihu describe Job?

Job 34:7-11

4.)   How does Elihu describe God?

Job 34:12-15

5.)   Explain God's justice to society.

Job 34:16-30

6.)   How does Elihu rebuke the statement that he used regarding Job?

Job 34:31-37

7.)   What questions does Elihu use to continue his argument?

Job 35:1-3

8.)   What is his response?

Job 35:4-7

9.)   How do our actions affect people, especially those who do evil actions?

Job 35:8

10.)   What action will pcoplc do and why?

Job 35:9-12

11.)   What is something God will not do in Elihu's view?

Job 35:13-16

PERSONAL QUESTIONS

A.)   Elihu often quotes Job. What does he use this time and why do you believe Elihu is using this technique?

B.)   Elihu used Job's statement against him, but slightly changed it. One of the times, he actually used a different person. Why do you believe Elihu did this for his rebuttal?

C.)   Do people often change their stories to fit their statement? Why would we do this?

JUST A THOUGHT

Elihu in his fervor or rush to correct Job tries to quote the man he's correcting. In some instances, he gets the idea of what Job is saying correct, but there are times when he gets the statement wrong. For example, Elihu says, "Do you think this is right? Do you say 'My righteousness is more then God's?" Job 35:2 NKJV. The real quote from Job is "…But how can a man be righteous before God? If one wished to contend with Him, he could not answer Him one time out of a thousand." Job 9:2-3.

The saying is sort of the same but slightly different. The problem with changing someone's words to fit your own arguments is that you could be wrong or very misleading. Sometimes that is done in the Bible from one character to another. For example, Satan tried to tempt Christ to commit suicide by quoting a scripture in Psalm. (Matt 4:5-6, Psalm 91:11-12). The Lord just used another scripture to counteract Satan, but still using the Bible for such a nefarious means is clearly wrong.

However, many people often change the words of their combatant or misquote other texts to make their point. For them it's all about the outcome and winning that particular battle or getting what you want from the person. It's not about being right, just convincing the other person you're right.

Be careful of how you categorize people or try to misquote scripture. Purposefully misquoting people means, you truly do not know the source or you're simply trying to control them.

God's Power

Lesson 23

Job 36-37

1.)   What does Elihu have to say about the legitimacy of his talk?
Job 36:1-4

2.)   What actions does Elihu give for God's character?
Job 36:5-7

3.)   How will God get people to change?
Job 36:8-10

4.)   What happens when a person obey and serve God? What happens if you don't?

Job 36:11-12

5.)   In Elihu's argument what do people with impure hearts/hypocrites do? What becomes of them?

Job 36:13-14

6.)   What will God do for the weak and poor?

Job 36:15-16

7.)   What warning does Elihu give?

Job 36:17-21

8.)   Describe God and His powers.

Job 36:22-33

9.)   God is known to have power with His voice. What acts is attributed to God's vocal command?

Job 37:1-12

10.)   Why does God use His power?

Job 37:13

11.)   Elihu talks with Job and continues his statement about God. What does he say and

        why do you believe he's using this as an example?

Job 37:14-20

12.)   What are Elihu concluding arguments?

Job 37:21-24

PERSONAL QUESTIONS

A.)   Looking over Elihu's comments to Job, how do you feel he stated his case? Do you believe it would have had a positive effect on Job? Would God be pleased?

B.)   To you what is the best way to help someone with words when a person is going through a calamity?

C.)   If someone is doing self-harm, what are ways you could help? What is something you could say to encourage them to change?

D.)   Give some characteristics of God that are important to you.

JUST A THOUGHT

A particular noticeable characteristic of Elihu, is either one of two things or possibly a mash of both, Elihu comes across supremely confident in his arguments or unbearably arrogant. Often it's a fine line that a person walk when coming across so bold. The moment the Bible introduces him, he's looked upon as someone with a lot of anger. He himself states this.

Sometimes with anger, it can cloud your mind and judgment. You have the idea of what you want to say but it cannot come out in a way that's helpful. Often times we believe that as long as words are coming out, then I've done my part. We never think of the personal feelings or emotions from our speech. Sometimes we will not consider the person's feelings we're talking to or trying to correct.

Read 1 Corinthians 13:1-3. It talks about being able to do astounding things but without a certain quality then it's not worth it. It literally profits you nothing. It was a waste of time. You do not want to be wasting your time because arrogance or a bad attitude got in the way of actually trying to help someone change from their bad behavior.

In addition, arrogance is a trait that often leads to pride. There is a plethora of different times in the Bible when pride is a terrible thing and causes many problems for everyone involved. Being confident in your words and abilities is great. It can lead you to overcome obstacles that might get in your way. However, arrogance can lead you astray from your goal and the very people you could have helped.

The Authority of God

Lesson 24

Job 38-39

1.) God comes and speak to Job. How is he portrayed and what does He say?
Job 38:1-3

2.) God immediately states His power and authority. In the verses below, write something that God is stating regarding His own power.
Job 38:4-7

:8-11

Continue on next page

:12-15

3.)   What are some of the questions that God has for Job?

Job 38:16-24

4.)   God continues to reveal His power and knowledge by using Earth and space. Next
        to the verse, write what He is referring too.

Job 38:25-30

Continue on next page

:31-33

:34-38

:39-41

Job 39:1-4

Continue on next page

:5-8

:9-12

:13-18

:19-25

:26-30

PERSONAL QUESTIONS

A.)   Why do you believe God calls the words of the men "dark counsel"?

B.)   Why do you believe God came to speak on His behalf to Job and his friends?

C.)   How do you feel God's description of Himself differ/similar to the men who were speaking about Him?

D.)   How does God communicate to you? It doesn't have to be as dramatic as a whirlwind or fiery bush, etc. It can be through a sermon, books, songs, voice in your mind, dreams…

JUST A THOUGHT

There are a variety of ways that God can communicate and show up to people. To Samuel, God came as a voice (1 Samuel 3:1-10), to Elijah, it was a voice but only after a few other phenomenon happened (1 Kings 19:11-13), and for Moses, it was in a burning bush (Exodus 3:1-6). In the past, messengers or angels were sent to relay God's message. For example, Abraham will have a mighty nation come from his loins (Genesis 18), Jacob's name was changed after wrestling an Angel (Genesis 32:24-30), and Gideon was given the message to save his people (Judges 6:11-22).

For Job, as you read, it was in the voice of a whirlwind. I would imagine nothing as overly destructive or powerful as a full fledge F5 tornado, but something that really caught the attention of the men that were there. For the Lord, it was a way of showing his power while holding their attention the entire time.

There are varieties of avenues the Lord can use to communicate with you. It might not be as fantastical as the burning bush, or for us now, our refrigerator being on fire, but not consumed. The way God communicates with you could be a small voice in your mind, through song, a sermon, a kind gesture by a stranger, or something you read on the internet. God can communicate countless ways with you. Listen, and just like Samuel, inform God that you're listening.

The Behemoth and Leviathan

Lesson 25

Job 40-41

1.)   What does God ask Job? What is He trying to say and imply?
Job 40:1-2

2.)   What was Job's response?
Job 40:3-5

3.)   God informs Job that He knows that there have been questions of the
       Almighty's justice. What acts does God ask if Job can perform?

Job 40:6-13

4.)   If Job could perform the act, what would God do for him?

Job 40:14

5.)   What animal does God use to reveal a small sample of His power? Describe the
       beast using at least three different examples or descriptions.

Job 40:15-24

6.)   The entire 41st chapter is dedicated to one animal. What is it and give five descriptions.

Job 41

PERSONAL QUESTIONS

A.)   Job was bold for most of the book in desiring a talk with God. When he had his chance to speak with God how does he present himself?

B.)   Why do you believe God chose these animals (Behemoth and Leviathan) to prove his point and show an example of His power?

C.)   God brings up a point regarding us believing to usurp His power. Why do we think we can usurp God and are there examples of society currently doing this?

JUST A THOUGHT

The two creatures represented in this section are up for debate. It doesn't mean that they do not exist, but concerned for what they are. Read some of the books in the Bibliography if you would like to see the multiple possibilities as to what they are. Many scholars believe that the Behemoth is either an Elephant or Hippopotamus with the latter being more plausible. In addition, they think the Leviathan was either a take on an ancient Crocodile, based off an Egyptian or Sumerian Sea Serpent, or a possible Dragon-like creature.

The truth is that it's tough because it's very possible that both animals existed during Job's time but are currently extinct. Various animals have existed and died within a few hundred years from today. As of now, there are probably animals living in forests and jungles that are dying off due to our expansion and growth across the World.

The Behemoth and Leviathan could very well be Dinosaurs or some other creature whose bones we have yet to come across. Then again, it could be an exaggeration on the Hippo and Crocodile. The idea isn't so much the animal themselves, but God's power over them.

For Job and his friends, God was showing that he ultimately has power over these two great creatures. It is He who keeps them in check, not people. It is God who created them for a purpose, and that people are not devastated by these beasts' magnificent power and strength. God wanted to show them that He is ultimately in control.

A New Beginning

Lesson 26

Job 42

1.)   After listening to God's words, what was Job's response?
Job 42:1-3

2.)   How does Job change? What is he willing to do?
Job 42:4-6

3.)   What did God say to Eliphaz, Bildad, and Zophar?

Job 42:7

4.)   What did God order the three men to do, and how was Job a part of the plan?

Job 42:8-9

5.)   What happened to Job after he completed the work God gave him?

Job 42:10-11

6.)   Describe Job's life and his possessions after the ordeal.

Job 42:12-17

PERSONAL QUESTION

A.)   Remember that at the beginning of the book, Satan wanted to tempt and harm Job. The entire time Job's friends were blaming him for his sins and God for putting Job through the situation. What does this say about their belief in who is responsible for pain and destruction?

B.)   In our current time, how do we regard destruction and calamites? Whom do we blame when bad things happen and why?

C.)   The Lord was not pleased with Job's friends for how they represented Him. What are ways that we can believe we're doing what is right but in reality not representing God according to His standard?

D.)   Gossiping, backbiting, or ruining someone's character is not spoken very often but is still an issue. As you read Job, his friends were not looked down upon by God for drunkenness, sexual immorality, or anything we normally call sin. They had to be forgiven for "dark counsel". Why would God look down upon people who are harming one another's character and name?

E.)   Job's family and fortune grew after he prayed for his friends. The same people who damaged his character and his name. How can we use this as an example to pray for all people (family, friends, and enemies)?

F.)   Why would God want Job to pray for the very people who scandalized his name?

JUST A THOUGHT

God wanted Job's life and suffering to be mention in the Bible for all those who would learn more about Him and life. The Bible is a map or a handbook to learn as much as we can about the character of God so that we will be prepared to live with Him in Heaven. Sometimes we believe that we can learn everything about God in the Bible, but in reality, it only reveals what the Lord wants us to know. While on Earth, we can never obtain the ability to learn about an omnipotent God. Our minds would breakdown and not be able to handle the amount of vast knowledge given to us.

Instead, God has authored the Bible through a variety of servants to reveal who He is. In the book of Job, there are varieties of things that we can learn. Job was a great man who suffered through no fault of his own and what he did against God. The Lord wanted to use a person who was good to teach all of us a few basic lessons.

First, God wanted to show that behavior does not necessarily warrant punishment or reward. Often we do pay for the consequences of our actions and do not have the license to treat people horribly. However, sometimes we believe there is a direct connection to every bad deed done to God or people. This isn't always true. The second thing, is that anyone can be touched by calamities or problems. It doesn't matter if you're rich or poor, your spiritual belief, race, gender, or your place of residence. All people will go through something and no one will be exempt from suffering. Last, your life, like Job, can serve as a way to teach others on how to endure. Job now serves as an example for us to hold on to God and believe. Ultimately, with God in control, your life will be greater in the end. More then you can imagine!

BIBLIOGRAPHY

Books

Alter, R. (2010). *The Wisdom Books: Job, Proverbs, and Ecclesiastes.* New York: W. W. Norton & Company Inc.

Balentine, S. E. (2003). *Mercer Commentary on the Old Testament.* Job, (pp. 405-430). Macon: Mercer University Press

Geisler, N. L. (1977). *A Popular Survey of the Old Testament.* Grand Rapids: Baker Books

Hinton, L. B. (1988). *Job: Bible Commentary.* Nashville: Graded Press

La Sore, W. A. & Hubbard, D. A. & Bush, F. W. (1982). *Old Testament Survey: The Message, Form, and Background of the Old Testament.* Grand Rapids: William B. Eerdmans Publishing Company

Larrimore, M. (2013). *The Book of Job: A Biography.* Princeton: Princeton University Press

Ross, H. (2011). *Hidden Treasures in the Book of Job: How the Oldest Book in the Bible Answers Today's Scientific Questions.* Grand Rapids. Baker Books

Horn, S. H. (2011). *The SDA Bible Commentary: Job*. Hagerstown: Review and Herald Publishing

Websites

White, E. G. (n.d.). Ellen G. White Writings. Retrieved March 21, 2015, from http://text.egwwritings.org/publication.php?pubtype=Book&booCode=3BC&pagenumber=1140

Bible Hub (n.d.). Book of Job. Retrieved March 21, 2015, from http://biblehub.com/job

Bible Gateway (n.d.). Book of Job. Retrieved March 21, 2015, from https://www.biblegateway.com/passage/?search=Job+1&version=KJV

Wikipedia (n.d.). Teman (Edom). Retrieved March 22, 2015, from http://en.wikipedia.org/wiki/Teman_(Edom)

www.ingramcontent.com/pod-product-compliance
Lightning Source LLC
Chambersburg PA
CBHW081537040426
42447CB00014B/3404